BRIGHT

KIKI PETROSINO

BRIGHT

SARABANDE BOOKS
Louisville, KY

Bright is a memoir. The events described in this book are from the recollections of the author as she experienced them. Dialogue may be reconstructed, but accurately reflects the author's memory and fairly conveys the meaning and substance of what was said.

Publisher's Cataloging-in-Publication Data
(Prepared by The Donohue Group, Inc.)

Names: Petrosino, Kiki, 1979– author.
Title: Bright / Kiki Petrosino.
Description: Louisville, KY : Sarabande Books, 2022
Identifiers: ISBN 9781946448927 (paperback) | ISBN 9781946448934 (e-book)
Subjects: LCSH: Petrosino, Kiki, 1979– | Women poets--United States—Biography.
Racially mixed people—United States—Biography. | Identity (Psychology)
Race discrimination—United States—History. | LCGFT: Autobiographies.
Classification: LCC PS3616.E868 Z46 2022 (print) | LCC PS3616.E868 (e-book)
DDC 811/.6—dc23

Cover design by Emily Mahon.
Interior design by Alban Fischer.
Printed in Canada.
This book is printed on acid-free paper.
Sarabande Books is a nonprofit literary organization.

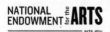

[clmp]

This project is supported in part by an award from the National Endowment
for the Arts. The Kentucky Arts Council, the state arts agency,
supports Sarabande Books with state tax dollars and federal
funding from the National Endowment for the Arts.

For my family

CONTENTS

THE MIRROR

You don't need white people's approval to be happy, the Mirror said. But if you want anything from their world, they have to like you.

Bright is an American slang term for light-skinned people of Black & white ancestry. It's not a compliment.

From an early age, I understood how *bright* applies to me, to my skin, to the face I show the world. I'm fair for a Black girl. Powdery-pale, especially in winter.

It's hard to love *bright.* The sly, knowing way its lone syllable sidles up. *Bright* gets too close too soon, thinking it knows all about me. To be frank, there's a mean smile in the word.

Light, bright, & damn near white, goes the rhyme.
Fuck those light brights, goes another.

As soon as I enter the classroom, as soon as I put my books on the lectern, as soon as I begin speaking, those who don't like *bright* don't like me, & I can feel it.

So what?

I was born in 1979, in Baltimore City, to a Black mother & Italian American father.

As Catholics (my mother having converted before my birth), they sent my sister & me to parochial schools.

At Immaculate Conception School in Baltimore, I turned the pages of a picture book about ladybugs beneath a bower of white-gold honeysuckle.

Some of the older girls taught me how to draw a single drop of nectar from the stem's fine filament & place it on my tongue.

Part of my Brightness begins this way.

In the mid-1980s, we moved to Shrewsbury, Pennsylvania, then a small, nearly all-white town just north of the Maryland line.

My parents built our new house in a development carved from seemingly endless farmland. Instead of a garage, they added an extra family room to our three-bedroom ranch house with its gray aluminum siding & burgundy shutters.

It was to be a house for sleepovers & summer barbecues, for holiday parties lasting far past bedtime. For months after we moved in, the house smelled like plaster, paint. The sharpness of fresh earth.

My parents loved southern Pennsylvania: its clear air, its country charm. It must have felt, to them, like an escape from the city. On weekends, they bought Amish potato rolls from the farmer's market & took us to nearby Dutch Wonderland, an amusement park composed entirely of kiddie rides.

What I remember: how the house spread horizontally across our quarter acre, while everything in Baltimore had been stacked high & close. Most of our neighbors in Shrewsbury were Catholic; we saw no other Black or interracial families.

Our Brightness was new, here.

4.

Here's how the plan for our family worked:

Each weekday morning, my parents got into the family car & commuted
an hour from Shrewsbury back down to Baltimore to teach in the
City schools.

My sister & I, in matching plaid uniforms, our braids tight on either side of
our heads, took the bus in the opposite direction, to a small Catholic school
where we were two of the only Black students in the building.

On the bus, we often held hands, even across the aisle, only unclasping
when another kid boarded.

From the bus windows, I would watch the dawn mist, its huge angelic
presence, rising from rural fields of green & manure-black. The barns
we passed along the road were decorated with the stylized goldfinches,
rosettes, & pineapples of the Pennsylvania Dutch.

What it meant: abundance, welcome, good luck.

When I first heard the name, *Pennsylvania*, I imagined we were moving
to a house made of pencils. We ended up in a suburb just emerging from
rural landscape.

Our street had no sidewalks, no parks or green space, only concrete gutters
leading to storm drains, each one stained orange with clay. Neighbor
to neighbor in this suburb, we glimpsed each other mostly through car
windows on our silent, collective way to Elsewhere: groceries, church,
the mall.

On summer nights, I could discern the promise of rain, as if it were a
feeling inside my body. Secretly, I would open my bedroom window,
touching my tongue to the metal screen. Crabgrass & vetch spread over the
backyard, like fists clenching & opening.

When he visited the ranch house that first year, my Italian grandfather
spent hours breaking up the stubborn clumps of reddish soil, heaving a
pick over his head & bringing it down for marigold beds.

Only reluctantly did the earth accept what we planted.

THE GARDEN

She looked down & noticed her own thighs: uneven fields, dug out with tiny spades.

6.

There's a loneliness in being called the N-word, in being called *zebra* & *darkie*, in rooms with saints' images on the walls, in spaces where we all prayed the rosary, bead by bead.

My sister & I forged a pact to get through recess: we would keep an eye on each other. If one of us ever saw the other alone, we would leave our game & come over immediately.

More than once, I remember my sister soundlessly appearing at my elbow, her face an orbiting moon of worry resembling my own.

For two weeks a year, on the hinge of summer & fall, my Italian grandparents would visit. Each of those days, Grandpa collected us at the bus stop, on foot, wearing his plaid flannel work shirts & jeans, fresh from the yard.

All the teasing, all the screaming taunts from the bus—they ended when Grandpa arrived. He walked us back to the house, slowly, in view of every neighbor on that street, each of his hands holding one of ours.

I don't know how to explain Pennsylvania, how it changed the story of my Brightness.

How I sat alone at lunch each day. How I started choosing the end seat, so as not to be marooned by empty chairs in the middle (I still do this). Back then, I believed in my own unworthiness as deeply as I believed in the Holy Trinity.

With a desperate pull in the chest—this is how I yearned for kindness from the teachers who lined us up on picture day. Teachers who, if someone's hair was out of place, would gently swoop it to one side with a plastic comb that was, then, that student's very own to keep.

When that teacher came to me—my hair erupting from its braids in a crazed halo—she would only sigh & say, "I'm afraid to even *touch* this," before turning her back.

Always, just at the edge of my vision, the white world burst into ecstatic blossom: girls sharing snacks & going to birthday parties, girls talking all night on the phone. I imagined what it would be like to go to a friend's house after school, the feeling of being gathered up, by a friend, into a sudden hug.

Decades later, my eyes still move across the calendar to the loftier girls' birthdays: April. May. June.

Abundance. Welcome. Good luck.

8.

When my sister & I drew in our coloring books, my mother always joined in, selecting crayons from our communal box.

I noticed how she filled every human face with complexity, blending brown & reddish shades, leaving the pale "flesh" crayon to languish alone. To flip through her coloring book was to glimpse a world full of variation. A place of tenderness & protection, where brown angels hovered over sleeping forest animals.

Late afternoons back then, I stood before the full-length mirror at the end of the hall & stared into its dim surface. Even before Pennsylvania, there was something I didn't like about my mouth, my teeth. It wouldn't go away.

Part of my Brightness begins here, too.

THE PROMISE

Yes! With all her heart, she must & would break open, & as for peril, she wouldn't be at all afraid.

9.

Once, in Pennsylvania, our school Christmas play was a retelling of
the Nativity.

I'd already learned how to escape into books & reading. Alone while the
others played, I slid from my body, not hearing or seeing anything but
Johnny Tremain, Anne of Green Gables, Little Women.

In this way, I became one Brightness.

10.

That winter, I memorized my lines & those of everyone else in the Nativity play. My own role, Narrator, kept me on my accustomed sideline: no costume, no scenes with the others.

But when the popular girl who'd been cast as Mary came down with the flu, my teacher told me to fill in. No one else knew the lines.

I held the box containing Mary's costume: the long white gown to wear over my uniform, & a textured blue cloth for a veil. I was going to be part of the story.

> *What? Who ever heard of a Black Mary?*

Later—could it have been the same day?—that same girl cornered me in the cloakroom.

> *K___'s parents spent a lot of money on that dress.*
> *You'd better not get it dirty. You'd better not ruin it.*

Of course, I already believed I could ruin it. I believed my body was capable of making clean things dirty & beautiful things ugly.

Each time I wore the costume, I made sure to place it back in its box, carefully following the original creases.

I imagined K___'s parents receiving the box at the end of the holiday season, wondering aloud if another child, let alone a Black one, really had worn the gown.

II.

At some point in my childhood, I started pulling out my eyelashes &
eyebrows. My mother called it a *nervous habit.*

I still do this to myself, in times of stress or uncertainty. I'll suddenly find
my thumb & forefinger pinching the arch of my eyebrow, getting ready
to pull.

When I talk about my Brightness, I must also talk about the fact that I have
reached, again & again, to harm my own face.

Why do I desire to feel each sharp, satisfying *zing*, that pain of
confirmation, as something tears away at the root?

THE MAIDEN

She felt her Brightness for the first time, when it turned & stood inside of her.

In 1771, Thomas Jefferson wrote of Monticello:

> *I have here but one room, which, like the cob[b]ler's, serves me for parlour,*
> *for kitchen and hall. I may add, for bed chamber and study too.*

What if my Brightness is a house? A place to enter—

Monticello, with its skull-white dome, the mansion Jefferson never
stopped dreaming.

In my journal, I write:

> *But when Jefferson dreams   he*
> *does not dream of me*

Jefferson begins *Notes on the State of Virginia* this way:

> Query I: *An exact description of the limits and boundaries of the State of Virginia*

Most of the first paragraph is a single sentence, set off with semicolons.

In this way, Jefferson divides Virginia from Maryland, Maryland from Pennsylvania, & the Algonquin town of Cinquac from the mouth of the Potomac River.

This is how he describes the shape of Virginia as it was in the 1780s:

> *an area somewhat triangular of one hundred and twenty-one thousand five hundred and twenty-five square miles*

A commonwealth floats up from the matrix of Jefferson's imagination: our Magic 8-Ball fortune.

Jefferson is the shadow I can't quite catch, hard white glint in the mirror of my own Brightness.

We both love(d) books. We both travel(ed) to France & Italy.

Jefferson's handwriting, in the margins of his personal copy of *Notes*, is surprisingly legible, flowing, alternately, in English, French, Italian, Latin, Spanish, & Greek. He writes in a small, rounded hand, each letter exactly the same size as the others.

There are times when my literacy crosses his, a sunbeam settling over the page in Special Collections—

THE COTTAGE

Her name meant *dweller*.

It was a name for dark places, for the shaded streams that course through the woods.

15.

My African ancestors arrived in Virginia in chains, on ships that maneuvered their way up the Rappahannock River from the Chesapeake Bay, & before that, from West African ports like Bonny & Old Calabar.

As soon as they step from the first ship, their African names surge back over the Atlantic, dissolving from my view. Jefferson's prose—his graphical tables measuring rainfall & the diameters of carriage wheels—draws a fine grid over the past.

Still—I crave to see my ancestors, in robes & crowns. I want to know if there's some message for me, stitched along the hems of their garments.

16.

In *Notes*, Jefferson is ravenous, too. His eyes range across the map, along each river. He searches for slugs of amethyst beneath the earth.

Jefferson's writing contains so much that I love about words: syntax, meter, image. In Query VI, trees coalesce into an elegant verticality of sound:

> *Black oak. Quercus nigra.*
> *White oak. Quercus alba.*
> *Red oak. Quercus rubra.*
> *Willow oak. Quercus phellos.*
> *Chesnut oak. Quercus prinus.*
> *Black jack oak. Quercus aquatica.*

A Jeffersonian catalog is more than a fixed container; it's a musical system that transmits his intentions.

Jefferson used his literacy to solidify the abstraction of Virginia. For whom did this place become real when he wrote it?

17.

Why do I want Jefferson's blessing?

Why do I want him to like me?

I wish he would wish me well in his six languages.

18.

In 1770, Jefferson argued before the General Court of Virginia on behalf of a mixed-race man, Samuel Howell, who had sued for his freedom on the grounds that his grandmother was a white woman. Jefferson wrote:

> *Under the law of nature, all men are born free. Every one comes into the world with a right to his own person, which includes the liberty of moving and using it at his own will.*

He lost the case.

But Jefferson would use this argument several years later, in the Declaration of Independence. By then, though, he would mean only white men.

In his public writings, Jefferson would insist on the inferiority of Black & mixed-race people, even as he fathered children with Sally Hemings, even as he relied on the people he treated as property to care for his house, his farms, his family.

19.

Scansion is the practice of measuring & describing metrical patterns in poetry, but you can apply its principles to any word.

In one of my favorite teaching activities, I have students scan their own names to find the music in them.

Thomas, for example, is a trochee because of its long first syllable & short final syllable.

The inverse of a trochee is an iamb, a pattern some believe goes back to the patterns of Anglophone speech, or even the da-dum of a beating heart.

But a trochee is a dancer. It has roots in the Greek term trokhaios pous, the running or spinning foot.

Thomas. Kiki. Thomas.

We know Jefferson suffered as he began writing *Notes*. In June 1781, the British invaded Virginia, forcing him to flee Monticello in the final days of his governorship.

Time wastes too fast . . .

Just a few months later, Martha Wayles Skelton Jefferson copied this sentence from her sickbed. The line comes from Laurence Sterne's *Tristram Shandy*.

Martha died from complications of her seventh pregnancy. There are no known portraits of her, only scraps of paper, like this one, bits of her handwriting which, Jefferson reportedly carried close to his person.

Did writing about Virginia help pull Jefferson up from sorrow?

Did he place his symmetrical catalogs, his marvelous litanies of plants & animals, against the solemn register of his losses?

Last time I visited Monticello, I stood at the door of a replica slave cabin & looked up & down the slope. From there, I could just see the main residence, a curve, half-hidden in the trees.

So many of my Black ancestors couldn't read or write. I know only pieces of their lives. Yet, in Virginia, their collective presence is very close to me, nearly palpable.

I think of this passage from Query VII of *Notes*:

> *Going out into the open air, in the temperate, and warm months of the year, we often meet with bodies of warm air, which passing by us in two or three seconds, do not afford time to the most sensible thermometer to seize their temperature. Judging from my feelings only, I think they approach the ordinary heat of the human body. Some of them perhaps go a little beyond it.*

THE WISH

No sooner had she whistled than she felt her Brightness rushing in from all sides, & such an assembly of Brightness shimmered down that it stunned all the meadow in which it settled.

Lately, I've been thinking about tenderness, how I wish it would break over me, like a spirit of air.

In Shakespeare's *The Tempest*, it's Ariel who warns the sorcerer, Prospero, that he must relinquish his anger.

In the world of the play, Ariel has no form. He's a nexus of language & feeling, the invisible arpeggio of a hummingbird's wing.

Ariel dips the ship, full of Prospero's enemies, beneath the ocean waves; he frightens the shipwrecked crew with eerie voices & visions that scatter them across the island.

Easy games for a spirit.

Yet, Ariel insists, if Prospero only allowed himself to see his enemies' sorrowful faces & hear their cries, *Your affections would become tender.*

Prospero is intrigued at this. *Dost thou think so, spirit?*

Mine would, Ariel says, *were I human.*

23.

My teacher Gregory Orr wrote in *Poetry as Survival*:

> *Even as we recognize the power of disorder in our experience, we are likely to become aware of a strong need we have to feel there is some order in the world that helps us feel safe and secure.*

Can belief, once planted, ever fail to attach itself to some elemental source? *Christ has died. Christ is risen. Christ will come again.*

The Old English poets sang in communal halls, sharing lines of alliterative verse. Repetition was meant to aid memory, but it also made the poems, like *Beowulf*, beautiful.

I love this beauty.

Ariel has no body.

Ariel has nobody, except for Prospero.

Only the sorcerer, arriving bruised & banished from Milan, rescues Ariel from the *cloven pine* where he was imprisoned by an evil witch.

Ariel has no body.

Confinement tortures him inside the pine. Those branches, so like human arms, upstretched, forked with pain.

Prospero tells him:

> *thou didst vent thy groans*
> *As fast as mill wheels strike.*

25.

My Italian grandfather's name:

Prospero

Prospero

Prospero

Prospero

Prospero

Prospero

Prospero

Prospero

Prospero

Prospero

Prospero

He was magical, just like the Duke of Milan, though born much farther south, in a stony village at the ankle of the Italian boot.

In America, Prospero gardened. He planted sweet william & *Portulaca*, moss roses, in our yard. Tiny, velvety flowers that unlatched from dark green buds.

Having grown up in Italy, his script was calligraphic & antique, his numerals swooping rightward, his letter *s* transforming into *f*, a musical curve.

In the only letter he wrote me, just as I set off for the University of Virginia, Prospero warned me against walking alone:

I *malviventi ci sono dappertutto.*

Evil ones are everywhere.

27.

One Tuesday morning, in the tenth decade of his life, Prospero hanged himself on the back of a door.

Years later, while unpacking books in my new house in Virginia, my mother finds this line by Sarah Manguso:

> *One must be able to empathize with a suicide yet not become one.*

What Prospero did is considered *a gravely evil choice* in Catholic tradition. For many years, I didn't tell his story.

I couldn't think of him as a wrongdoer, *un malvivente.*

At the funeral, as I watched the priest wreathe his casket in long strands of incense, I seemed a visitor at some ancient ceremony.

My affections refused to become tender.

28.

I lost the letter.

THE SPELL

She rubbed her eyes & wept till the world looked blue.

29.

In the thirteenth canto of *Inferno*, the Anonymous Florentine Suicide
weeps before Dante.

The soul of the Suicide has become a thorn tree. When Dante breaks off a
twig, its speech gushes forth, in jets of words & blood:

Io *fei gibetto a me de le mie case.*

Here is a shade of stifled grief, confined within cells of bark & wood.

I recognize these trees, *i malviventi*, ink-black, lifting their brittle limbs
from the soil.

I *made my house into my gallows.*

Out of love, out of love—

Dante gathers up the Suicide's twisted branches & all its black leaves,
which grow no flowers.

30.

Someday I'll tell you of the hours I spent with *Inferno* in my hands, searching, again, for that thorn tree.

31.

I'll break my staff.

I'll drown my book.

THE QUESTION

She shook the last swan rib from the sleeve of her gown & used it to pry open the keyhole.

Oh, oh! cried the Door. *Why did you open me?*

32.

If, in separating from the church of my birth & early education, I'm no longer rooted in a living theological tradition, then willful rootlessness must be my state.

Mostly, this suits me.

I can imagine my soul as the wild briar where tenderness refuses to grow.

Within poetry is a kind of divinity, one that requires me to listen, with my human ears, to its human voice.

As the poet reads, I connect to their deep humanity, & to the language that enacts the poem's quest.

I, too, am on a quest.

33.

I don't understand every psalm, but I want to be a psalmist.

About a year before his death, I heard Seamus Heaney recite his poem "Digging," a masterpiece about labor & identity.

As Heaney announced the title, excitement rippled over the London crowd. It was like the first moments of a rock show, when you recognize the notes of your favorite riff.

"Digging" is beautiful. In the *curt cuts of an edge*, Heaney finds solace & the resolution to keep writing.

I've always envied Heaney's ability to root down into multiple traditions of belonging: culture & poetry; faith & poetry; country & family & poetry.

Yet. As much as I miss the communal experience of the Catholic liturgy, some part of me twists away from its neat trellises.

I won't divide my vestments into purple & green, my calendar into Days of Obligation & Ordinary Time.

35.

Prospero said: *On the Other Side, I made locks.*
Every day I worked next to a big fire.

I made the very best locks, all of iron.
Nobody could beat me.

36.

My Brightness spirals around my losses, thorn & blood & briar.
I cannot change this.

A beautiful passage in Hebrews describes Abraham & his family going

to live in the land of promise, as in a foreign land.

To live in faith means being a stranger to many of this world's concerns,
particularly its material encumbrances.

To write a poem is to assert one's attachment to the materiality of language,
but it also requires the poet to assume the openhanded posture of a
questioner.

I have words, & I have questions.

37.

One summer, in Pennsylvania, Prospero painted shut my bedroom window, smoothing over the exact seam I used to open to let the rain in.

Other times, I watched him split the soft green flesh of a pear with a small knife.

He would prize out a pale wedge & hold it out to me, translucent, balanced on the blade.

38.

I've never wanted to kill myself. But there have been times, in my life, when I've wanted to be with the dead.

THE DEPARTURE

Are you afraid? asked her Brightness.

No! She wasn't.

39.

The Wood of the Suicides is a forest of flesh, the only place like it in all
Inferno. It breathes & bleeds.

Having murdered themselves, having tried, violently, to separate body from
soul, each Suicide is flung upon the soil of the Wood, where

    it fastens like a seed.

After the funeral, I went back to school in Virginia. At a discount salon in
Charlottesville, I had all my hair buzzed to a quarter of an inch.

I liked how hot the top of my head always felt, now, when I pressed my
palm against it.

How sharp the bristles of my natural hair, too short for curling irons
& relaxers.

In Italian, you don't turn off the light. You *close* it, only to *open the light* again
in the morning.

40.

In describing the bewildering sounds of the Wood, the pilgrim Dante appears to stammer with astonishment, but the careful music of his *terza rima* never fails:

> *Cred' ïo ch'ei credette ch'io credesse*
> *che tante voci uscisser, tra quei bronchi,*
> *da gente che per noi si nascondesse.*

The *c* & *s* sounds make a series of sonic knots, like howls & yelps twisting into one cry.

I go back over the passage as I once prayed my rosary beads, pronouncing the syllables, one by one, in their original order.

41.

Years later, at the train station in Naples, my cousin greets me by first imitating Prospero's voice.

My skull expands in recognition of the sound, calvarium from mandible, as if my bones were held together with golden pins.

Sunlight opens above me & I decide to stay.

THE KEY

Do you really think you can show yourself before the world? asked the Sea Witch. Why, you have nothing but the Brightness you stand in!

42.

What did I ever want from the white world?

43.

Early evening in Louisville: I'm invited for dinner at the home of a white friend.

She rents a converted carriage house at the rear of an elderly woman's grand estate.

Louisville has many grand estates, & elderly white ladies, & carriage houses.

Oh, my people have been here for years & years

the gracious lady says, raising her elegantly braceleted arms,

I'm a thoroughbred.

44.

On my first day as a Professor of Poetry at my alma mater, another new, white, professor presses her arm against mine.

That afternoon at orientation, I'd asked about the percentage of students of color in the entering undergraduate class. Smaller, I'd noted aloud, than when I'd attended as a Black student some twenty years earlier.

After orientation, on our way out of the meeting room, this white woman presses her arm against mine & says she appreciated my question from earlier.

> *Even though I'm darker than you.*
> *I'm a lot darker than you.*

45

What I don't like about my Brightness: how it gets to be a surface where others feel invited to view themselves.

In others' gazes, I lose my privacy, just as the moon does, reflecting.

Think of the moon on her way, her mind unraveling the mystery of herself, but never truly alone, on account of everyone below, pointing out the faces they think they see in hers.

My inheritance smiles out from my skin. Here are my narrow jaws & coiling hair. I look like the women on both sides of my family. Not all dark. Not all light.

You know, from my Brightness, exactly how I was made. It's not a private story.

I think that's what you don't like about me.

THE RIDDLE

She was lucky to be born when & where she was.

She knew this.

46.

The problem is

my white poet friend says

women & African Americans can never be sure if they've really been hired for their talent, or just to check a box. There's just no way to really, really know

& you have to live with that.

47.

Once, after a poetry reading, a white woman suddenly reached for my curls, scrunching them in her two hands. She said

I've been wanting to do that all evening.

Briefly, her arms framed our faces, cutting off my peripheral vision & pulling me into her intimate airspace.

I remember my surprise, like an invisible yolk dripping all through my insides, at this idea of

all evening.

Before she'd put her hands on me, I hadn't been thinking of her at all, & now, years later, I can't forget this woman.

48.

Does the moon consent to being watched?

Does she permit the sun's gaze, or simply tolerate it?

When the moon touches her tongue to the inside of her own cheek, what secret flower does she draw there?

49.

In poems, I've described my color as

   a high & disagreeable gold.

My Brightness is a friend, it is a friend.
I feel about it just as my Black grandfather would say of himself:

   I'm a good color.

He always sat in the front row for group portraits at the War Department,
where he worked, mostly, with white men.

We have portrait after portrait of Ralph Harrison Beverly: business suit,
pale pocket square, brown smiling face.

I am good, too.

THE PRINCE

When they went to bed on their wedding night, he asked again where her Brightness was, for he said, *Now we're married, you must show it to me.*

50.

Once upon a time, two people wished to grow their family, so they sent copies of their chromosomes into the deep, dark forest.

Once upon a time, two people wished to grow their family, so they sent copies of their chromosomes into the deep, dark forest.

There, in a clearing, their child began

Once upon a time, two people wished to grow their family, so they sent copies of their chromosomes into the deep, dark forest.

There, in a clearing, their child began **to take shape, her limbs & organs following the contours of each ancestral gene.**

Once upon a time, two people wished to grow their family, so they sent copies of their chromosomes into the deep, dark forest.

There, in a clearing, their child began to take shape, her limbs & organs following the contours of each ancestral gene.

Certain proteins switched on

Once upon a time, two people wished to grow their family, so they sent copies of their chromosomes into the deep, dark forest.

There, in a clearing, their child began to take shape, her limbs & organs following the contours of each ancestral gene.

Certain proteins switched on, **while others subsided.**

Once upon a time, two people wished to grow their family, so they sent copies of their chromosomes into the deep, dark forest.

There, in a clearing, their child began to take shape, her limbs & organs following the contours of each ancestral gene.

Certain proteins switched on, while others subsided.

The world named one parent Black & the other white, but

Once upon a time, two people wished to grow their family, so they sent copies of their chromosomes into the deep, dark forest.

There, in a clearing, their child began to take shape, her limbs & organs following the contours of each ancestral gene.

Certain proteins switched on, while others subsided.

The world named one parent Black & the other white, but **neither set of genes originated in just one earthly place.**

Once upon a time, two people wished to grow their family, so they sent copies of their chromosomes into the deep, dark forest.

There, in a clearing, their child began to take shape, her limbs & organs following the contours of each ancestral gene.

Certain proteins switched on, while others subsided.

The world named one parent Black & the other white, but neither set of genes originated in just one earthly place.

This was a secret   **the child's body remembered.**

Once upon a time, two people wished to grow their family, so they sent copies of their chromosomes into the deep, dark forest.

There, in a clearing, their child began to take shape, her limbs & organs following the contours of each ancestral gene.

Certain proteins switched on, while others subsided.

The world named one parent Black & the other white, but neither set of genes originated in just one earthly place.

This was a secret **the world forgot,** but the child's body remembered.

Once upon a time, two people wished to grow their family, so they sent copies of their chromosomes into the deep, dark forest.

There, in a clearing, their child began to take shape, her limbs & organs following the contours of each ancestral gene.

Certain proteins switched on, while others subsided.

The world named one parent Black & the other white, but neither set of genes originated in just one earthly place.

This was a secret the world forgot, but the child's body remembered.

In each of her cells, continents merged & drifted

Once upon a time, two people wished to grow their family, so they sent copies of their chromosomes into the deep, dark forest.

There, in a clearing, their child began to take shape, her limbs & organs following the contours of each ancestral gene.

Certain proteins switched on, while others subsided.

The world named one parent Black & the other white, but neither set of genes originated in just one earthly place.

This was a secret the world forgot, but the child's body remembered.

In each of her cells, continents merged & drifted

ancestor

   child

      ancestor

Once upon a time, two people wished to grow their family, so they sent copies of their chromosomes into the deep, dark forest.

There, in a clearing, their child began to take shape, her limbs & organs following the contours of each ancestral gene.

Certain proteins switched on, while others subsided.

The world named one parent Black & the other white, but neither set of genes originated in just one earthly place.

This was a secret the world forgot, but the child's body remembered.

In each of her cells, continents merged & drifted

     ancestor
         child
            ancestor

More than twenty thousand ancient stars deliberated on the child's gifts

Once upon a time, two people wished to grow their family, so they sent copies of their chromosomes into the deep, dark forest.

There, in a clearing, their child began to take shape, her limbs & organs following the contours of each ancestral gene.

Certain proteins switched on, while others subsided.

The world named one parent Black & the other white, but neither set of genes originated in just one earthly place.

This was a secret the world forgot, but the child's body remembered.

In each of her cells, continents merged & drifted

        ancestor

              child

                    ancestor

More than twenty thousand ancient stars deliberated on the child's gifts
before settling, at last

Once upon a time, two people wished to grow their family, so they sent copies of their chromosomes into the deep, dark forest.

There, in a clearing, their child began to take shape, her limbs & organs following the contours of each ancestral gène.

Certain proteins switched on, while others subsided.

The world named one parent Black & the other white, but neither set of genes originated in just one earthly place.

This was a secret the world forgot, but the child's body remembered.

In each of her cells, continents merged & drifted

      ancestor
             child
                  ancestor

More than twenty thousand ancient stars deliberated on the child's gifts before settling, at last, **on all**

Once upon a time, two people wished to grow their family, so they sent copies of their chromosomes into the deep, dark forest.

There, in a clearing, their child began to take shape, her limbs & organs following the contours of each ancestral gene.

Certain proteins switched on, while others subsided.

The world named one parent Black & the other white, but neither set of genes originated in just one earthly place.

This was a secret the world forgot, but the child's body remembered.

In each of her cells, continents merged & drifted

> *ancestor*
> > *child*
> > > *ancestor*

More than twenty thousand ancient stars deliberated on the child's gifts before settling, at last, on all **she would carry.**

THE MIRROR (II)

Never leave me, she said
I'll never leave you.

NOTES

The twelve "fairy tale" interludes are inspired, in part, by *East of the Sun and West of the Moon: Old Tales from the North*, illustrated by Kay Nielsen. I refer to the 2008 Calla Editions republication of the 1920 original American edition published by George H. Doran Company, New York.

4: Don Yoder & Thomas E. Graves's *Hex Signs: Pennsylvania Dutch Barn Symbols & Their Meaning* (Stackpole Books, 2000) is an excellent resource for learning more about the iconography of Pennsylvania Dutch folk art.

12: The quote is from Thomas Jefferson's letter to James Ogilvie dated February 20, 1771.

14: Thomas Jefferson's personal, hand-annotated copy of *Notes on the State of Virginia* (1787) is held by the Albert and Shirley Small Special Collections Library at the University of Virginia.

15: For the geographical information pertaining to the routes of Virginia-bound slave ships, I refer to John Randolph Barden's 1993 dissertation from Duke University: "'Flushed with Notions of Freedom': The Growth and Emancipation of a Virginia Slave Community, 1732–1812." My maternal grandfather's ancestors (surname: Harris) were part of the free & enslaved communities investigated in Barden's work. The reference to "robes & crowns" comes from Revelations 4:4.

18: The case is *Howell v. Netherland* (1770).

20: A digital copy of the note is available on the Library of Congress website: https://www.loc.gov/exhibits/jefferson/images/vc26a.jpg.

23: The quotation from Gregory Orr comes from his introduction to *Poetry as Survival* (University of Georgia Press, 2002). The refrain "Christ has died, Christ is risen, Christ will come again" is part of the Memorial Acclamation in the Roman Missal.

27: The quote from Sarah Manguso comes from her book *300 Arguments* (Graywolf Press, 2017). The phrase "a gravely evil choice" comes from Pope John Paul II's 1995 Encyclical *Evangelium Vitae*, section 66.

29: The quotation comes from the Robert & Jean Hollander translation of Dante Alighieri's *Inferno*, canto XIII, line 151.

31: The quotations come from Prospero's speech in Shakespeare's *The Tempest* act V, scene i, lines 63 & 66.

34: Seamus Heaney appeared at London's Southbank Centre as part of the 2012 Poetry Parnassus festival.

36: The quoted line is from Hebrews 11:9.

39: The quotation comes from the Hollander translation of *Inferno*, canto XIII, line 99. The original line reads: *quivi germoglia come gran di spelta.*

40: The quoted stanza is from *Inferno*, canto XIII, lines 25–27. I have quoted the Italian original as it appears in the Hollander translation.

49: The quote is from my poem "Mulattress [6]," published in *Hymn for the Black Terrific* (Sarabande Books, 2013).

ACKNOWLEDGMENTS

Parts of this work have appeared, in earlier forms & under different titles, in the *Iowa Review* & online at *Tin House*, *Ploughshares*, & the Poetry Foundation's *Harriet* blog.

Other portions of this work began as conference papers I presented at the 2017 Lines & Spaces Summit, sponsored by the University of Iowa's International Writing Program, & at Calvin University's 2018 Christian Poetics Symposium.

Many thanks to the National Endowment for the Arts, to the University of Virginia's College of Arts & Sciences, & to the UVA Department of English for their support of this work.

KIKI PETROSINO is the author of *White Blood: A Lyric of Virginia* (2020) and three other poetry books. She holds graduate degrees from the University of Chicago and the University of Iowa Writers' Workshop. Her poems and essays have appeared in *Prairie Schooner, Best American Poetry, The Nation,* the *New York Times, Fence, Gulf Coast, jubilat, Tin House,* and online at *Ploughshares.* She teaches at the University of Virginia as a Professor of Poetry. Petrosino is the recipient of a Pushcart Prize, a Fellowship in Creative Writing from the National Endowment for the Arts, an Al Smith Fellowship Award from the Kentucky Arts Council, and the University of North Texas Rilke Prize.

SARABANDE BOOKS is a nonprofit literary press located in Louisville, KY. Founded in 1994 to champion poetry, short fiction, and essay, we are committed to creating lasting editions that honor exceptional writing. For more information, please visit sarabandebooks.org.